D1556535

THE EXECUTIVE DIRECTOR OF THE FALLEN WORLD

PHOENIX **POETS**

LIAM RECTOR

{ The Executive Director of the Fallen World }

THE UNIVERSITY OF CHICAGO PRESS
Chicago and London

LIAM RECTOR is the founder and director of the graduate
Writing Seminars at Bennington College. He is the author of
two books of poems, *American Prodigal* (1994), and *The Sorrow
of Architecture* (1984), the editor of *The Day I Was Older: On the
Poetry of Donald Hall* (1989), and co-editor, with Tree Swenson,
of *On the Poetry of Frank Bidart: Fastening the Voice to the Page*
(2006). He lives in New York.

The University of Chicago Press, Chicago 60637
The University of Chicago Press, Ltd., London
© 2006 by Liam Rector
All rights reserved. Published 2006
Printed in the United States of America

15 14 13 12 11 10 09 08 07 06   1 2 3 4 5

ISBN-10: 0-226-70604-4 (cloth)
ISBN-13: 978-0-226-70604-7 (cloth)

Rector, Liam, 1949–
  The executive director of the fallen world / Liam Rector.
     p. cm. — (Phoenix poets)
  ISBN 0-226-70604-4 (cloth : alk. paper)
  I. Title. II. Series.
  PS3568.E29E96 2006
  813'.54—dc22

                                            2005025322

for Tree Swenson

for Virginia Rector

The opposite of love is not hate, it's indifference.

— ELIE WIESEL

Where does the skin end?

— ALFRED NORTH WHITEHEAD

*Find those with whom you have rapport and proceed. And never proceed
with those with whom you do not have rapport.*

— RUDD FLEMING

All's misalliance.

— ROBERT LOWELL

I is someone else.

— ARTHUR RIMBAUD

Contents

Acknowledgements

The author gratefully acknowledges the editors and publishers of the following periodicals, in which these poems first appeared:

American Poetry Review: "About the Money," "Always," "Back to Country with Pulitzer," "Ever Upon the Gad," "Family Plot," "In My Memory Eddie," "Jack Warden," "Off to the Country of Cancer," "Song Years," "Third Star with Guggenheim"

Boston Phoenix: "The Worry of the Far Right"

Columbia: A Journal of Literature and Art: "Soon the City"

Cortland Review: "So We'll Go No More"

5 A.M.: "Beautiful, Sane Women," "Corner Man"

Pif: "I Get a Feeling," "Larkin," "The Old Man and the Motorcycle," "Your Tales of the Suburbs"

Ploughshares: "Now," "Our Last Period Together"

"Ronald Beaver's Life in England" first appeared in *AGNI 55*.

"Best Friend" first appeared in *AGNI 61*.

"One for the Guys and for Robert DeNiro" and "Peyote" reprinted from *Boston Review*.

"When the Parents Went" first appeared in *The Gettysburg Review*, volume 15, number 1, and is reprinted here with the acknowledgment of the editors.

"This Summer" first appeared in *Slate.com*.

"In My Memory Eddie" is for Susan Cheever, "Song Years" is for David Daniel, "Your Tales of the Suburbs" is for David Fenza, "Best Friend" and "Peyote" are for James Haft, and "Handmade Shoes" is for Askold Melnyczuk.

Many thanks to Victoria Clausi, David Fenza, Donald Hall, and Tree Swenson for their critical readings of the manuscript, and thanks also to David Bonanno, Lucie Brock-Broido, and, as always, to Rudd and Polly Fleming.

THE EXECUTIVE DIRECTOR OF THE FALLEN WORLD

In My Memory Eddie

Great-Uncle Eddie
Came to see us in the country.
Eddie looked exactly

Like Fred Astaire, floating
Fred Astaire (and Eddie
For some reason had on

A tuxedo, top hat, and spats).
I loved Eddie.
At eight I was already

Gone to the movies,
And Eddie looked exactly
Like a world just beyond,

Like a well-lit city just over
The hill. (I could not imagine
How Eddie came out of anything

Resembling our family.)
Eventually
Eddie hanged himself: just kicked out

The stool beneath him and, after
What I imagine was a brief struggle
On a lonely day for Eddie, Eddie

Was gone. And when I asked
My grandmother what would make Eddie
Do such a thing, she, in a moment

Of uncharacteristic candor,
Said Eddie simply could not stand
Getting older. I did not know it

At the time, but Eddie
Had already transported me
(Much as Astaire transported,

Much as startling art transports)
Towards the city, no matter
How much I loved the country.

(My grandmother said before I left
She could understand how I felt
About Eddie, and she apologized

For allowing me to so often sit up late with her
And experience
What she suddenly called

"Too many movies.")
And now that I live
In New York City,

Where nights
Of top hats, champagne,
And limousines actually are

Part of life, I, when really dressed,
Always raise a glass to Eddie.
I raise a glass to Eddie and to a time

When men believed so deeply
In style (or at least in
Their clothes) (or at least in the movies)

That when those men died (at least
When they chose to exercise
The option of ending themselves

By hanging)
They had the decency,
Before they kicked out their stools

(And I have documentation
To support this),
They had the damned decency

To make sure
They died with their hats on.
And these days I find

My greatest transport (outside
The movies, where I still live)
By remembering such days

As when Eddie
Came to visit us
In the country.

Now

Now I see it: a few years
To play around while being
Bossed around

By the taller ones, the ones
With the money
And more muscle, however

Tender or indifferent
They might be at being
Parents; then off to school

And the years of struggle
With authority while learning
Violent gobs of things one didn't

Want to know, with a few tender
And tough teachers thrown in
Who taught what one wanted

And needed to know; then time
To go out and make one's own
Money (on the day or in

The night-shift), playing around
A little longer ("Seed-time,"
"Salad days") with some

Young "discretionary income"
Before procreation (which
Brings one quickly, too quickly,

Into play with some variation
Of settling down); then,
Most often for most, the despised

Job (though some work their way
Around this with work of real
Delight, life's work, with the deepest

Pleasures of mastery); then years
Spent, forgotten, in the middle decades
Of repair, creation, money

Gathered and spent making the family
Happen, as one's own children busily
Work their way into and through

The cycle themselves,
Comic and tragic to see, with some
Fine moments playing with them;

Then, through no inherent virtue
Of one's own, but only because
The oldest ones are busy falling

Off the edge of the planet,
The years of governing,
Of being the dreaded authority

One's self; then the recognition
(Often requiring a stiff drink) that it
Will all soon be ending for one's self,

But not before Alzheimer's comes
For some, as Alzheimer's comes
For my father-in-law now (who

Has forgotten not only who
Shakespeare is but that he taught
Shakespeare for thirty years,

And who sings and dances amidst
The forgotten in the place
To which he's been taken); then

An ever-deepening sense of time
And how the end might really happen,
To really submit, bend, and go

(Raging against that night is really
An adolescent's idiot game).
Time soon to take my place

In the long line of my ancestors
(Whose names I mostly never knew
Or have recently forgotten)

Who took their place, spirit poised
In mature humility (or as jackasses
Braying against the inevitable)

Before me, having been moved
By time through time, having done
The time and their times.

"Nearer my god to thee" I sing
On the deck of my personal Titanic,
An agnostic vessel in the mind.

Born alone, die alone—and sad, though
Vastly accompanied, to see
The sadness in the loved ones

To be left behind, and one more
Moment of wondering what,
If anything, comes next . . .

Never to have been completely
Certain what I was doing
Alive, but having stayed aloft

Amidst an almost sinister doubt.
I say to my children
Don't be afraid, be buoyed

—In its void the world is always
Falling apart, entropy its law
—I tell them those who build

And master are the ones invariably
Merry: Give and take quarter,
Create good meals within the slaughter,

A place for repose and laughter
In the consoling beds of being tender,
I tell them now, my son, my daughter.

Back to Country with Pulitzer

I left here at eight
And returned at 75.
In between

I largely wasted America.
I married, had children,
Distinguished myself in a profession

Full of fools, becoming one myself,
As is the way
Of this (or, I suppose, of any other) world.

I missed
The Nobel but I did bring down
The Pulitzer. The weather,

The politics, the stars,
And my own small contribution
All lined up, and I got one.

So "Pulitzer" became my middle name
Before I came here, where no one cares
A whit about such things.

I failed at love.
That's where I truly fucked up.
I couldn't.

The women in this town
Are mostly severe, resentful
—The men bitter, disappointed:

A perfect place for my purposes.
I stay in a room
In the house of an old woman

Who doesn't want to have sex any more
And neither do I
So we do not

Trouble each other on that front,
Which is good.
I do like to drink.

I used to love to eat
But then I don't much
Give a shit

About any of that now.
The old woman sometimes says wistfully
God will soon be calling both of us

Back home, but as an agnostic
I don't believe that.
As an American,

I don't buy that.
I came here to retire from love,
To face my failure to love

As I attempted to face everything
Else before, and that
Is exactly what I am doing and doing

With the exactness I used to put into
My work, for which I received the Pulitzer.
I hate a coward.

My son
Came here the other day and asked
Exactly when I might

Be coming back
And I sent him off without an answer.
The answer

Seems to be staying here,
Staying honestly here and coming to terms
With my greatest single failure.

My wife is dead. To me,
It seems I am left over
To eat a shit sandwich.

"Eat me," the world says,
Now that I have lost my appetite.
We used to say, "Eat me"

To each other in high school,
Another thing from which no one
Ever recovers. America likes to think

Every one can recover from every thing,
But about this,
Especially, America is wrong.

Song Years

For years I lived in a kind
Of wistful song world where
One foot was always out

The door, almost like a sailor
Ready, anxious even, to decamp
Once more for the sea,

And always the American highway
And its great story calling, built by
The American restless and all

Its subsequent moving. Loosely
Around the seasons I moved
Looking for what I thought of

As a natural life, and looked back
At anyone who stayed put as if
They had given up,

Given up something
That should never be
Given up,

Ever.
No sooner
Would I get some place

Than I'd begin
To check out the train schedules
And other venues of departure.

I hated the notion
Of insurance and never
Had any. I gave

Myself no place to fall.
I thought of all this as keeping
Myself clean, keeping

Myself honest. It really
Wasn't a variant
Of the old high school

Locker-room chant of find 'em,
Feel 'em, fuck 'em,
And forget 'em, I told myself,

But sometimes,
Especially when I was packing,
It surely felt that way.

I was always leaving one
For the next one. I wished them
Well and remained friends

With most of them. I hoped
A right one would come along
For them, and they would be

More ready for their lasting lover
Given the lessons, good and bad,
We'd taught each other.

Fall would come
And I'd head north
For apple-picking, winter

Would find me holed up
In Vermont for a moment,
Working on some chilly construction,

And spring was always
A sure-fired scamper south.
Summer mostly meant

Going out west for, I suppose, hope.
Change is slow and hope is violent.
I wanted the speed and handling

Of a good sports car; I wanted
Things not as they should be
But things as they are.

Most songs are sad and most people
Do not want to live in song world,
Except when some loved one leaves

Or maybe over a drink, alone, at home,
Or perhaps in a car, ever more alone.
Someone is always falling or being thrown.

Most songs say
But one thing:
"My heart aches,"

And if you doubt this
Listen to the songs.
And tonight

Let us all together send out
Our love to the songwriters
For moving us.

I moved this way
Until the cruelty of it
Overwhelmed me.

In Memoriam: (Harriet)

What to say about Harriet?
As her close friend for 30 years
(Harriet had the gift for friendship,

For intimacy, for confidences,
For love), where to start?
Harriet suffered

From Obsessive-Compulsive Disorder
And nothing, particularly not
The most common and everyday

Thing, was ever easy for Harriet.
The sunny-side of all these
Fletchings and crypto-manias

Was to behold the tics and twists
Of Harriet's clothes (Edwardian,
Neurasthenic, flowing), not to

Mention her interior decorating
Derangements: To witness her incessant
Draping of herself and her world

Was to get an utter eyeball
Crammed with beauty. Harriet,
Consenting minx, was beautiful.

(Comely breasts, fine waist, eyes a' fire.)
Harriet was also hysterical. Harriet
Did as much as anyone can

To counteract the panics and shakings,
The conniptions and mind-searing superstitions
In the DNA of (shall we say?) hysteria

Itself (after all, Harriet was born in a brown paper
Sack in Detroit and adopted by-and-by
By a wealthy family in Chicago). Harriet's story

Was an uncommon one, though not without
Precedent in the class in which Harriet
Grew up (though "growing up"—and Harriet

Would be among the first to stress this
—Was never among Harriet's strong suits).
Adoptive father a swashbuckling rug merchant,

Mother a force of culture as well as nature,
Nature a driving sexual force in, of course,
The very barnyard of reality and its getting-up-

On-each-other beauty. . . And the constant slippage
Of beauty inherent in the stampede of the aging body
—Beauty lost only to the untrained eye

—Was another of Harriet's horrors. Harriet
Preferred the swaddling innocence and body
Of the first year of childhood and did everything

She could (Harriet always a hopped-up fan
Of the impossible) to preserve that first year,
First World state in herself (and, it must be said,

Accomplished much in this mode). Some
Of the particulars of Harriet's bio: trust
Fund, insomnia, not eating, dread. Harriet

Wore mostly slips in the public high school
She attended, decades before
Victoria's Secret made its mark

(Though Elizabeth Taylor had by then played
Her eye-popping part in popularizing hanging out
In slips, most notably in the films *Cat on a Hot*

Tin Roof and *Butterfield 8*). Harriet
Was sent to several psychiatrists and even
To an early mental institution (much like

Taylor in *Suddenly, Last Summer*), so
Insane was it to wear slips in the halls
Of the high schools of that time,

And Harriet, as we well
Know, never abandoned a kind of
Sartorial insanity (which was,

If the truth be told, her splendor).
Insanity itself, in fact and in fable, followed
Harriet wherever she went. (Harriet driven

To the hospital in slamming snow late night
To be admitted for the night, into the night.)
Insanity was a kind of muse and phobia-frolic

For Harriet (had she been from the South
This would have been much more fully
Absorbed, largely in the Blanche DuBois

And in the Southern homosexual tradition),
And once you were around Harriet for more
Than 15 minutes all this madness

Was perfectly obvious (which it was, as well,
With my mother, who shall remain the subject
For some other memorial). Madness tends

To seep out mostly from the mouth—which
Was sometimes, as we all know, the case
With Harriet (Harriet yak yak with always

A startling admix of the high and the very low),
Though there are always many other modes
Of seep other than the mouth (I see a ton

Of seepage as I stare out upon all you now).
But now, and I'll try and come to some point here,
Harriet's hours are done

And we all gather amidst each other tonight
To speak of Harriet and endings
(And, having no other choice

When one speaks, to speak also of ourselves),
And to speak slant of the sloping madness,
The hysterical hill down which life careers . . .

Fair Harriet. Bloomsbury Weeper
Who could have found true company
In all those Edwardian sitting rooms,

Life good and gone for Harriet . . .
Harriet lived to be much older
Than ever Harriet thought

Possible, and I, for one,
Will remain rueful about
Being left to live a moment longer

Without Harriet. Without Harriet
And her singular take-no-prisoners humor,
Always tendered with a certain

Goofballness, it will be more difficult
To suffer the world's and my own
Foolishness, the absurd prima donna

In all of us, and our own general psychotic
Venality . . . Enough said about that.
Presence, immaculate presence:

One of the things Harriet had.
The way Harriet looked at it:
People aren't all that bad.

Life passed for her the way
Life passes for the major artists:
Insanely (or is this just a romantic

Truffle?). In any case, Harriet was truly
One of the ones: Harriet, obsessively alive,
Obsessively done now, mercifully done

With herself, down for the count,
Doused (and about 15 minutes now
Before death comes for

The horrid, whinging rest of us).

Sarcastic Caustic Ironic Satiric Sardonic Funny: Wounding Poetry

Was
A question of tone
And values, philosophy

And how
People were at the time.
Not liked,

Her work,
And barely tolerated when
It came to the publish.

Did not
Provide the sentimental bath
Of the seeming-to-empathize

Warm human humanism
(Which meanwhile wondered
What you might look like

In a coffin)
So peculiar
To her time.

(Blurbs in her day
Over and over,
With utter and

Unexamined vanity,
Said, "Above all,
Deeply human.")

Did not
Insist you see how
Sensitive she was.

Did not,
To her and to
Most people's

Horror, identify
With anyone. In fact
Put identity aside

As a deluded con,
A self-stroking hustle,
The fiction of a single

Or group self
With no singularity.
So struck many

As mean, misanthropic,
Wet with contempt,
And something best

Dismissed as being
In league with
The demonic, however

Well some of it
Might be stated or shaped.
Was not

Self-improvement,
And the dwindling
Number of readers

Wanted definitely
Not to inhabit. Old tragedians
Found it

Hilarious, young nihilists
Got their kick out
Of it, but its darkness,

Deep-fried in rue
(As took place all through
Her being),

Was not
Somewhere people
Generally

Wanted to dwell.
Drove them lulu.
Gone to hell.

Had wit,
But then
Most wanted

Nothing
To do
With it,

With its kind
Of shit:
Pooh-poohed it.

But lived it.

Disgust

I was well towards the end
Of middle-age before I
Realized I loved saying

Disgusting things but didn't
Really myself much enjoy hearing
Them. They

Go to the heart of life,
I realize (I think
Everyone recognizes this),

Since almost everyone
Can agree: Life, so
Generally disgusting.

But no one really
Wants to hear
That much about

The disgusting (except,
Perhaps, those who have frozen
Significant portions

Of their senses of humor
In the fifth grade, as I have).
Those of us who love

Verbally bringing up
The disgusting
Incessantly

Are usually prevented
From ever holding
Truly executive positions

In any organized
Situation, but there are,
Looking around I've noticed,

Plenty of us
Placed somewhere
In middle-management.

We are the ones
Managing things
"On the ground,"

As they say, the ground
Which is also where,
I can't help but bring it

Up, most beasts of the field
Leave
Their ghastly deposits.

When the Parents Went

When my parents,
Who separated
When I was four,

Died roughly
Within a year of each other
Last year

—She on one coast of America,
He on the other (boxers
To their corners!)—

I felt lightened
And folded
Towards myself, quietly,

Where someone laughed loudly,
As I'd heard sometimes happens
To sons and daughters

At funerals.
I think my half-brother, step-
Brother, and half-sister expected me

To cry at the memorial ceremony
For my mother, but I didn't.
I felt solicitous

Of other people's mourning, but otherwise
I felt wonderfully, maturely
Brutal—in full throttle, really.

That side of my family
Spent a night together
Before I left, a night

With the photograph album,
And when we came to
The picture of Mom's marriage

To my father, whom no one else
In the room really knew, everyone
In the room was duly dazzled

By how miserable Mom looked
In the photo. It had been a shotgun
Wedding, occasioned by me,

There already
In Mom's belly, six months
Before I, unwanted, came to be.

Now that she was gone
They were both gone, and there
Seemed no way in hell

They could ever again reach me
In the same way, which seemed
So good to me. It was over.

The long arc of unwant was over,
And all we all did trying to come to terms
With unwant—an impossibility—

Was ended
With their going,
Which was more

Than I ever dared
Hope for. That time
Of the three of us worrying

That bone—that DNA, that inherit,
That mistake made way back
In the 1940s—that time

Was blessedly over, and only I
Was left over to make
Whatever could be made of that folly.

Mental Mommy

Home from school at six years old, first grade,
And uncle there to tell me Mommy
Gone, Mommy not be coming back any

Time soon, Liam, Mommy had to go to
Mental hospital. Nervous breakdown.
Years later Mommy, when she gets out

Of mental, often says, "If you're
A bad boy for me Liam you're
Going to send me back, back

Into mental hospital, like you did
First time." At 13
I find out Mom had been doing years

In a federal prison all that time,
For stealing, so no mental hospital for
Mommy. Breakdown ours alone.

I was on my one.

The One at the Oars

My father, that bastard,
Was always trying
To tell me things I'd

Remember once he was
Gone, and now that he's gone
I go back fondly mostly

To the times when he was silly
And made faces or took on
The face and voice of some

Outrageous character.
I also remember
The day we rowed out

On the Chesapeake Bay
And a storm came up
And he told me to take

Our small boat back to land.
The waters started coming over
Both sides of the boat,

And no matter how hard I
Rowed nothing
Seemed to gain us an inch.

My father, who wasn't a man
Much given
To such things, kept repeating

A line from a poem he knew,
A line about "The captain's
Troubled mind." And now that I

Am in charge of the world
I often summon that line,
And think about how the old

Bastard gave me my stead that day,
Taking his direction from his son's
Line-making business in this world.

Family Plot

Once taking LSD I went back
To revisit at night
The old home our family had

Just vacated. A sign
On the side of the house said
The house was now

Owned by the FBI
(My mother having recently fled
Across state lines in order

To avoid prosecution
On an embezzlement charge).
That night

I sat in the backyard
Behind some bushes
(Careful to make sure no one

Could see me) and imagined
The former life of my family
Alive in that house:

Lights came on suddenly
In the bathroom
As family members,

In turn, went in
To brush their teeth,
Preparing for sleep.

I knew my family
Was far away, though I'd not
Been told where

They were, in case
The FBI came by
(As my mother thought might happen)

To shake me down
About the family whereabouts.
The drug and I both

Conjured the family there
That night one last time,
Putting them

Through their nightly rituals
One more time.
Goodnight, goodnight,

My heart said as I watched,
And I then turned
To the swing set

My brother and I
Had once so carefully
Put together

For my sister,
And to a few of her toys
Still strewn and shining

With an almost happy brightness
On the grasses
Of that suburban lawn.

I buried them all there
That night, right there,
With the help of the powerful

Hallucinogen I was
Then using frequently
In a strenuous effort

To try to change
The fate of what I then
Called my mind.

Your Tales of the Suburbs

Your father's middle-aged, dog-like,
Dionysian friend in the suburbs
Who underwent heart attack and realized

None of the rich, high-living, caloric bounties of nature,
Food nor drink nor tobacco,
Could ever be his again,

And so waded
Out into a pond on his property
And shot himself in the head with a .22 pistol.

He, quite neatly—elegantly, even, from my perspective
—Knew that if the .22 didn't get him
The drowning water of the pond would.

You were my friend in youth, you are
My friend in middle age, and the chemo
We both had last year gave us

A very bad taste of what it will soon be like
To be so old and weak and dizzy
That the younger cows seem to be pushing us

Around on the sidewalks, but we made it back
And settled, for the moment, into Middle Age.
As it turned out

We don't live in the suburbs
But live instead in the city.
You came in

From the smelt furnaces of Pennsylvania
And I from the farms of Virginia.
Money is putting the squeeze on us.

You in Washington now, me in Boston,
And talking with you over the phone this morning
Wondering where we'll go for dinner,

Wondering where my daughter might go
For college. With you, childless so far,
And neither of us ever far from thinking

About the man
With his .22, about up to
His chest in water in his pond.

Handmade Shoes

So here I am,
Here I go walking
In Liam's shoes,

The size twelves
I inherited
When Liam died.

English tan, lace-up,
Cap-toe shoes,
Beautifully aged.

How fitting
To have them and to
Go in them, given

That going was Liam's
Real subject. He in fact
Thought of little else.

People die,
Babies are born,
And it is good to take up

A dead man's shoes,
Liam's transport,
Walking my way

Through the world without
My friend, afloat
In the very fine shoes

He was known
For buying, meant to last
A lifetime.

That boy paid
A price for living
The way he lived.

Expensive
Life,
Expensive shoes.

The Worry of the Far Right

The Reverend Donald Wildmon, executive director
Of the American Family Association of Tupelo,
Mississippi, birthplace of Elvis Presley, Elvis who

Unleashed the libido of a generation, announced today
That he, the Reverend, wanted again an America
In which he could drive his convertible into town,

Park it, leave his keys in the ignition,
And worry only that it might rain,
Rather than worry about Liam Rector.

Who's in Charge of the Culture Now?

From The Patriarchal Prick
To The Evil Nanny, much
Less fun now. We hoped for greater

Tenderness, intuition, mercy,
Less violence, but got leftist
Margaret Thatchers, less humor,

Less drinking, cursing, spitting:
Things make life worth living.
Nanny, Nanny, tut-tutting. Orgy

Of revenge, resentment,
Suffocating many, Nanny . . .
What we got was the chilling:

No one honestly
Saying anything, what we got
Was safety over adventure

And the censor every day,
Security over the wild
Every night. Meanwhile

Sheer terror
On the right . . .
Bush the dry-drunk

Patriarchal Prick,
C-student frat rat,
America The Evil Empire:

No real excuse either.
Two wrongs make no right.
Only thing left of the left:

Evil Nanny.

One for the Guys and for Robert DeNiro

I was the young psychopath Travis Bickle
In *Taxi Driver*, and I am now the aging one,
Middle-aged gangster, hair-slicked-back

Jimmy Conway in *GoodFellas*. DeNiro
Not pretty, not the early Brando, not James Dean,
But DeNiro who gets the fucking guy job done.

DeNiro's aging mobster maturity keeps guys
Like me going now. American guys, tough
Guys, guys afraid of the world and women

And their place in both. Guys ready
To jack some serious jaw if it comes
To that, guys ready to go to jail if jail

Is preceded by doing the right guy thing,
Guys coming up through the ranks,
The hard way, guys who don't like dinner

Parties but do like to sit down and eat
Like animals. Like pigs. Like a dog
Guys, guys who don't put much store

In houses, guys who dream only of cars always.
In typical disguise, guys tough on the outside
And guys who are always mush and shit

And "Stella!" inside their guy. Inside me,
I see now, is a pantheon of American film boys,
But none so real, none so solid as the DeNiro guy.

He the one who represents us in France,
Inside, in everywhere-else-in-the-world; he our
American guy, up through the ranks,

Did it the hard way, American guy guy.

Corner Man

You took that round,
Champ! You didn't
Just sit and pout:

Now get the hell
Back in there
And knock the fucker out.

Jack Warden

In a Woody Allen film
A physicist
Played by Jack Warden

Says to Sam Waterston,
Both of them
Sitting out

On the porch of a house
In New England
One summer night

—While putting
A very stiff drink
Into his mouth

Jack Warden, a wonderful
Character actor, says the universe
Is for him "Haphazard,

Morally neutral,
And unimaginably
Violent." Seems

That way to me,
And once Warden puts it
That way I recognize

That truth immediately.
And seems it's all
There, everything

I've really needed
To know since
I was a boy,

A very young boy
Come to sit there
By himself in the theatre,

All there
In the movies
If I would but

Go in there
And look
And listen for it.

Larkin

The most even-
Tempered man
Ever known:

Always in a rage.

Third Star with Guggenheim

My former father-in-law Frank
Was getting his third star as a General
And the rest of the family and I

Were there and a Colonel dressed up
In a special-occasion all-white uniform
Walked around with a hand-mic singing

Sinatra's "My Way," and when he finished
Singing the Colonel said "His way" was how
Frank had done it all, all the way here to this

Glorious night of Frank's third star,
And Frank I think liked the guy
And appreciated the singing but Frank

Romped right up to the rostrum and said
He hadn't done it his way at all
But had in fact done it

"The Air Force way." (Frank was
The kind of guy despised by
Ruggedly individual writers. Frank was

A "team player.") One could almost
See the balls of the Colonel
Shrivel, and I realized no one

In the room thought
The Colonel would ever
Get to be a General now.

That's the way it goes
There in the Air Force.
One gets "passed over"

At the time the General
Appointments are being passed
Out. We in the family

Were all seated at the same table
And suddenly a spotlight was thrown
On our table. We were all

Introduced and the announcer said
I was that year a "Guggenheim
Fellow," which I was that year, and I

Remember thinking, "No one
In this room has the first fucking idea
What a Guggenheim fellowship

Actually is," but it was the snob
In me thinking and I found I was wrong
When several people came over later

To congratulate me and I noticed
Some in this wild crowd
Actually did recognize

The brand names
Of the rich
In America.

Woman in the Summer Southern Night

So depressed I thought
Sleeping outside under the stars
Might do something to put

A dent in the biochemistry
Choking me, making me forget
Anything that might make life

Worth living, I went outside
To sleep but found it too
God-damned hot to sleep even

Out there under the stars.
And still I could not find sleep
When a woman came

Screaming from the place
Out back of ours—"Lord, God,"
She said, "I didn't mean

To do it! Lord God I didn't mean
To do it to him Lord!"
She went on like this,

Making it all the way
Out to the highway, screaming
This way all the way.

Almost a half hour of this
Until the highway patrol
Pulled in, followed shortly

By the coroner, and finally I got up
And found the woman
Had chopped her husband's

Head off with a hatchet, which
Struck me, a young boy
Unable to find sleep, even

Out there under the stars,
Way out there, come from my room
To try and sleep some,

It struck me,
Given the humidity,
As something almost inevitable.

Fat Southern Men in Summer Suits

Fat Southern men in their summer suits,
Usually with suspenders, love to sweat
Into and even *through* their coats,

Taking it as a matter of *honor* to do so,
Especially when the humidity gets as *close*
As it does each Southern summer.

Some think men could do better
By just going ahead and taking the damned
Coats off, but the summer code stays

Because summer is the time
For many men, no matter what their class,
To be *Southern Gentlemen* by keeping

Those coats on. So late in life here I am
Down here again, having *run* to fat
(As Southern men tend), visiting the farm

Where my grandfather deposited
So much of his own working sweat,
Where Granddaddy never bought into any

Of "that Southern Gentleman crap."
Up north where I landed in the urban
Middle class I am seldom caught

Not wearing a coat of some kind. I love
The coats, and though I love them most
In the fall I still enact the summer code,

I suppose, because my father and I did buy
That code, even though I organized students
To strike down any dress code whatsoever

In the high school I attended (it was a matter
Of honor). And it still puts me in good humor
To abide with the many pockets, including

One for a flask. So whether it's New York,
Vermont, or Virginia, the spectacle
Of the summer seersucker proceeds,

Suspenders and all, and I *lean* into the sweat
(Right down to where the weather really is)
Until it has entirely *soaked* through my jacket.

Twenty-three

When he was 23 and beautiful
He liked to hang around
With other beautiful people.

He liked to get intoxicated with them,
Have sex with them, make money
With them. Among them,

He found, one did not have to strain.
Other people
Wanted to hang around with them

And came bearing gifts,
A little something. (These
Gift-bearers were a lot like

Politics itself is, "Showbiz
For ugly people.") In this world
If anything went wrong there

Was always enough money around
To cover it. After he was through
With this crowd he started hanging

Out with a bunch of academic
Gangsters. These were
A different crew altogether:

Smart, on the main, but mean
And eaten alive by resentment.
They never had enough money

And were bitter beyond belief,
Compared, say,
To a troupe of electricians.

Freud said somewhere
In our unconscious
We are always 23.

Twenty-four

Through the middle years
We took on the burdens
Of accomplishment mingled

Mightily with the sex-sauce
Of money. I didn't think
For an instant

About what to do
About getting a job
In the future

We've come to
Until I was exactly
24 years old. I remember

The moment,
On a balcony
In Adams Morgan

In Washington,
D.C., my hometown.
I sat with you,

Who held
A bachelor's degree in philosophy
And worked then

In a fish store, so great
Your love of fish. I loved books
So I staggered out of college

And worked in a bookstore.
We knew at 24 on that balcony
Unless we found other jobs

We'd be in
The badly paid nine-to-five store
Of retail (unless we actually owned

The store) for the rest of our lives, so
We actually let loose the thought
Of getting "real jobs." And in this

Instant of concession we knew something
(Youth?) (Fucking
Around?) was ending.

We knew something was passing
From our lives. We knew
The animals we'd always been

And wanted to be were passing
From our lives, that we
—Philosophy, fish, and books

In tow—had just thought
The thought we'd been avoiding
For 24. You went

Into computers (which paid
For a string of startling, staring
Saltwater fish-tanks at home)

And I, in years of unforgettable
Poverty and moving constantly,
Took too long finding work

Finally in the life of letters.
A good thing for us both actually,
To find the work, because

The children were soon with us.
And now that even middle age
Slips from us with utter rapacity,

We two old raptors sit on a terrace
In the Manhattan
To which I've come,

Our own children
Only a few
Years from 24 now.

They'll repeat that moment
On their own balconies, and youth
Will soon thereafter

Slip from them.
Jobs: youth-enders.
Work: the stuff of life.

San Francisco 1970, Years After the Summer of Love

For a time I viewed myself as a "street person"
And one night I was of course on the street
With a girlfriend, a blonde from Los Angeles.

We'd come on up to San Francisco because
We thought it looked a lot like Europe and wasn't
Quite as trashy and dependent on the car as was

Los Angeles. We couldn't afford (and didn't want) a car.
We were two young sorts looking for some action on
The streets that night, when two Mexican guys saw

That look in our eyes, held out a bottle of wine and said,
"Want some?" We did. We wanted and had some.
We were completely prepared to have more and then

Move on again out through the night, perhaps accompanied
By our new friends, whom we thought were a couple
Of animate, lively, game, and generous sort of street people.

And then one of the guys, the old one, suggested we go up
To their hotel room and have some more wine up there.
We looked at each other, the blonde and I, and we thought,

"What the hell, we're street people," and also thought
It might be worth our time to get in off the streets and spend
Some time in a genuine street people sort of dive hotel.

So we went, and it was a genuine dive hotel: urine stains
On the lampshades, two junkies in the next room arguing
About which one had managed to steal the most TVs,

And who, therefore, was to get the lion's share of the shot.
And soon in this Hotel of Lost Light the drinking recommenced
And the blonde and I thought this entire thing was really pretty

Cool, pretty much what we came up from L.A. for,
And then the old guy called me out into the hall
And asked me how much I wanted for the blonde.

She and I also believed in free love at the time so I
Told him he'd have to ask her about that, that
I wasn't a pimp. (That was part of the street life

I hadn't gotten around to yet.) The old man got pissed
And went off to the john in the hall and called to his
Young pal to come join him for a brief discussion.

Apparently at the conference the old man confided
In the young man that his plan was to beat me senseless,
Rape the blonde, and then throw the two of us back

Out onto the streets where we could go on being "street
People," which we told him we were when we first met
The two of them. But the old one had first to take a crap

And the young one bolted back promptly and told us
We'd better get out, get the hell out right away, that when
The old man got drunk he could get meaner than shit,

And that he, the young man, didn't want to see two people
Like ourselves get really fucked over. I said maybe we could talk
To the old man and convince him that free love was better

Than the kind of violent shit the old man had in mind,
And the young man looked at me incredulously and told me
Again to get the hell out, really get the hell out, if we valued

Our lives at all. It was a moment of solidarity
Between youth, a thing not so uncommon in those days.
So we left pronto, confiding to each other when we

Hit the street that we were disappointed street people
Couldn't practice a code among themselves, and also
Practice the vagaries of free love, the kind of vagaries

We then lived by. We didn't say anything else that night
But the next morning over breakfast in a greasy spoon
We spoke of the fact that maybe no one could ever really

Trust anyone, that perhaps even she and I could not
Really trust each other, and it wasn't long after this
That we broke up with each other. We "split"

And I then went off to college "back East," while she stayed West . . .
And the last time I talked to her, years later, liquored-up and late
One night, she told me she, Joyce, was making a living

As a stripper—no, not really as a stripper, she said,
But as someone who sat in a small stall and conducted
"Nude encounter sessions" for guys who came in off

The street, the street where we two young people had
Once sought solidarity in our lust for experience of the young
Sort, in the time when someone had to completely betray you

In order to take away the romance of something as public
And possible as the streets. The streets where we were then convinced
A revolution was taking place, where the nation was in the midst

Of a wild new change and, looking back, there was something
Of a wild new change taking place, of the cultural sort, though not
Of the economic sort, which is what makes any real revolution

A real revolution, but economics was something about which
We then knew nothing, though it is now something I've learned
A ton about, since working like a horse in torn harness.

Best Friend

You sailed down
From Provincetown
And I was to meet you

In Key West. I'd never
Sailed. I dressed
In my best and flew

Down from Manhattan,
Where I had been feeling
Punishing failure

And reading Hart Crane.
I brought a robe
I intended to wear

When I jumped off
Our boat mid-sea. I never
Told you that,

Old friend, and I
Apologize now.
What if I had left you mid-ocean

To sail alone?
In our 20-foot wooden
Thing with no motor

And a radio that didn't
Work we barely made it
Through the initial storm.

In the Bahamas we
Were often stood
Free beers for being

As insane as we were,
Coming over those waters
With no motor, pure

Sailing like that, a bar
Of soap floating in the cauldron
Of the Bermuda Triangle,

Where motorized cigarette
Boats sped by at money-making
Speeds, running drugs to fill

American needs.
And on our way back
When we lost our rudder

You, former Eagle
Scout, first conscientious
Objector ever to leave

West Point, captain
Of the ski team, jumped
Over the stern

And fashioned out of oar
And thick rope the thing
That would see us to shore

Before we, becalmed,
Drifted off course
100 miles, 100 miles

Of boredom and sun. I snapped
A black and white photo
Of the sea to remind me

Of my boredom, its boredom.
We made it back
To America, hitting

Shore at Boca Raton,
Pulling in midst the boats
Of the very, very rich.

I lived to write this
And never jumped ship.
It was your kinship

Kept me going those years,
Times of ridiculous
Sailing, riotous beers.

Wives sailed by,
So many boats, and you soon
Left for Bangkok and its

Very distant coast.
Being young: being rich
Among inherited ruins.

Peyote

Amidst Americans celebrating
Labor Day in the Bahama islands
(Vulgar, we thought, in their

Cabin cruisers, compared
To our small wooden sailboat
With no motor), we took peyote

And no one thought anything
Of our barfing off the side
Of our boat, which truly got

The peyote going. (Many
On other boats were really
Drunk and doing

More or less the same vomiting.)
As the sun went down
The other boats left and we went

To shore on the small island.
You migrated to the side
Of the island teeming

With thousands of life forms
In the small crags
Of the watery rocks

While I drifted over
To the side with the dead brain coral
Where it looked as if everything

Had happened and stopped happening.
We could barely hear each other calling
From our two sides of the island.

We could see
The differences
In our characters

There, you siding
With the living
And me taking

Communion among the dead.
(We knew peyote had taken us
To the shores of myth.)

I was soon to teach
At a prep school
And I resolved to teach

Your side of the island
As Lawrence and my side
As Eliot, teaching literature

As something of
A living island
With its own

Cemetery side.
It was to be my first post
Teaching, and I was going

Out of my mind to find
Something to say
To those young faces.

You were by then
A veteran teacher, a natural
Teacher. You could

Step into any room
And teach any thing.
Peyote was the one doing

The teaching that night,
And we submitted and gambled
With our minds hoping

We might find something to take
Back to America, something
Beyond even where the boats go.

The Old Man and the Motorcycle

The old man had inoperable cancer.
The old man's wife was dead
And the old man's kids didn't like him,

So the old man sold most everything
And bought a motorcycle
And the old man got back

To the backroads, to the roads he'd so
Enjoyed as a young man,
And the old man figured what the hell,

I'm sick I don't have long I might
As well die falling off this thing
Somewhere: this affordable, this moving,

This very roaring thing on these last roads.

About the Money

By the turn of the century
Talking about the money
Replaced talking about the sex,

Talking about one's so-called
Religious life, and all that
Earlier yak about the psyche.

Talking about the money
Got down to it and captured
The hunger, the hope,

The love, and the fear:
Let me hear your money talk,
Many sang.

Money was a good time
(What people want most is
Good times and insurance?)

And money picked up
The garbage the following
Morning. (Someone's

Got to do it and someone gets
Money to *do it*.) There was
Really nothing like talking

About the money if you wanted
To really get to know someone,
To get to know what animated,

What moved the American.
Do me. Do it to me, honey.
Do my money. Let's get cynical:

Let me hear your money talk.

Ronald Beaver's Life in England

Here drifted
An hedonist.

Life in England for Ronald Beaver.
Old London house in England with dog
For Ronald Beaver. Job in publishing

And old fart day spent in park beavering.
Gone in gum for Ronald, sweater boy.
Wife gone, beans straight out of can,

T.S. Eliot and Byron's "So We'll Go
No More a Roving" keep Ronald's mind
Nimble so Ronald can remember go pee

In all of England, in most of Tennessee.
Ronald Beaver move on boy to your last
Days now, put off nurse home, and raise

Your left leg and really blast one,
Merry olde Ronald. All gone to shit now,
As Ronald knew would, gone to

Hardly-remember way down under the sea.
No big deal for you Ronald, you Beaver,
You so much like Bette Davis now Ronald

And no sissy, she. Ronald lean back and let
What's left of mind go to music, starting with
The empty report a gun makes when shot

Over sea. Rapport, Ronald, rapport. Only music
Can give it to you now. You're balled-up,
You're frightened, you half-way through the door.

Remember: *Hedonism* means dog-like,
And stay true to the dog in you
Ronald, because the dog is true.

It's a big piss in a big sea, it's a real pisser
To have to go out but it's true, and now Ronald,
Our Ronald, O Ronald, O England—go pee.

I Get a Feeling

I get a feeling of discomfort, pressure
In my rear end, and I know then
It's again time to shit. This has been

Happening every day now
For 55 years, 55 years
In which the waste of life

Has been steadily moving.
I keep time this way now.
I wait for the feeling and then when

It does come I do its bidding.
I wait for the sex pressure and when it comes
I go where it says go.

I get somewhat the same discomfort for fame
And I leave the happiness of my study
To mortify myself one more time.

Off to the Country of Cancer

It comes on.
Comes on with the word,
A doctor's word,

The doctor saying *cancer*.
"But do I have cancer?"
"Yes, cancer."

Doctor has to say cancer
One more time
Before the cancer

In me
Becomes the word
I give over to it.

"What then
Will we
Do?" (A *we*

Enters
Quickly, to calm
The *alone*

Setting in
Quicker,
And then I

Let go of the *we*
Altogether.)
"We'll do

A regimen of chemo
And radiation and hope
For the best." "Well, that

Sounds like something. You're sure
I have cancer?" "Yes,
Cancer, that's it."

This Summer

Sitting in the chair that is somewhere
Between the chair of a barbershop and a beauty parlor,
Chemo dripping into the catheter

Surgically implanted into my chest, into body,
I resolve to smoke at least a half-ounce
Of marijuana when I get home.

Perhaps I'll smoke a pound.
Dizzier than hell must be dizzy,
I'm still able to drive

(Though will I be able next week?),
And after getting my ticket punched
I roar out of the Farber Clinic

(How splendid to have cancer in Boston
And fall heir to the astute care
Available here)

In the silver sports car I drive
During this debacle,
And heat roars into me

With humidity so deep
It is a theological offense
Which I cannot help

But take personally.
I think I may die without god,
My single comic integrity

That I *have* remained
An atheist in the foxhole,
Though I am ready

To roar through the gates
If there are gates.
This summer I've joined the grown-old,

The infirm, the shut-ins, and the bald-headed young
(They the hardest to bear), this summer
Starting with chemotherapy and ending,

By god it seems almost an ending,
With thirty radiation treatments
Which have brought me to my knees.

The marijuana works. It clears things.
How lovely!
How lonely it is sometimes to have cancer.

The grass is as good as it was
When I was 16 and found grass made the grass
A bit greener over yonder.

Almost as good
As the music I listened to that summer.
This summer I rejoin

The ever-new and always refreshing
Get naked and stay stoned Baudelairian crowd
As I plop stoned on the many rocks

Of a river in Vermont
Next to my friend's house
Where we have for so many summers

Worshipped the backroads
With the sports cars the two of us have driven
Since we got the money to get them.

With the top down I have worshipped this summer
The songs I've recorded on tape,
Driving and listening incessantly,

Thinking this may be my last summer
This summer. This summer
I have conversed with death every minute

And found out I have the talent
To submit, to leave, even to flee,
And, in this, there's nothing exceptional

About me. Why, the sidewalks around Farber
Are populated with so many about to die,
Many of great courage and grim humor and great shuffle,

Getting ready, as they can, to go,
Looking like they do, like the wounded of Atlanta
Lying around in Atlanta just after the burning

Of Atlanta in *Gone with the Wind*.
I am among them.
They are mine and I am theirs.

Our motto: Fight to live; prepare to go.
This summer it is so good
To hear from friends (one of whom I hear

Just died: brain tumor) before I drive on out
For another burn of radiation,
Before I suit myself with another week of chemo

Tied to a portable belt so I can go out
Easily to the ocean, to remaining
Friends there, before I lean into another joint,

A late-century life afloat on a sea of loans,
And hear over the telephone my sixteen-year-old
Daughter in Virginia saying she now thinks

She will never ever smoke marijuana
Because it is, after all,
Just another "gateway drug."

First Marriage

I made it cross-country
In a little under three days.
The engine blew out

About a hundred miles north
Of San Francisco, where I'd
Hoped to start living again

With a woman I'd abandoned
Only a few months before.
The reasons I'd left her were

Wincingly obvious
Soon as I got back
To her, and it didn't take long

Before I again left her.
In a few weeks I'd meet
The woman who became

My first wife, the one
With whom I spent
Almost the entirety

Of my twenties. It took
About twenty years
Getting over her, after

We divorced at thirty.
Broke then, I took
A bus cross-country

And was back in the East
By Christmas, thinking it
Would take three years maybe

To put this one behind me.
But getting over her
Happened as we were

Both in our third marriages,
Both then with children,
Heading for our fifties.

She came cross-country
To tend to me when I had
Cancer, with a 20% chance

Of recovery. The recovery
From all she had been to me,
Me abiding with her as long

As I did, took place finally
When we, her sitting on my bed
And me lying in it, held hands

And watched ourselves watching
TV, something we'd never quite
Been able to do comfortably

All those years ago. So many
Things turn this way over time,
So much tenderness and memory,

Problems not to be solved
But lived, and I resolved
Right then to start living

Only in this kind of time.
Cancer gave this to me: being
Able to sit, comfortably, to get

Over her finally, and to
Get on with the fight to live while
Staying ready to die daily.

Beautiful, Sane Women

I could have married rich
Several times, and married
Beautiful, sane women

Who adored me.
No strain.
But I strained

To get out of things,
Each time with each
One. One morning

I'd wake up and leave,
Just to throw chaos
Into my life one more

Time, in what struck me
Then as The Nick of Time,
Time to get back

To the chaos I took myself
And the world to be.
The trash. Towards

What I heard the French
Call *The impulse*
Towards the gutter.

Looking back I wonder
What the hell those
Beautiful, sane women

Must have thought
Was happening. What
Was happening was

I was on script
Betraying poverty
And then betraying

My need to betray
Poverty, poverty
Put in me so deeply

As my family early
Shifted around endlessly,
Leaving me,

I thought, with no choice
Other than to be
Some kind of Gandhi.

Ever Upon the Gad

She said she could not
Love him because he
Was ever upon the gad.

Our Last Period Together

Lying together in bed we feel soon
We'll do what's right and end
The wrong thing we've come to be,

I to you, and you to me.
Not all of it, as it turned out,
Was wrong. Year one,

Year two . . . And perhaps
In honor of that time we make love
One more time, something we've

Mostly stopped wanting to do,
You to me, and I to you.
After you've climaxed and I'm

Coming along, you lean back
—No pills, no diaphragm, nothing—
And take that sperm right into you.

This much we give over to fate
In case we're wrong, in case
We shouldn't be separating, in case

We should stay. And then as soon
As your period comes, two weeks later,
I go away.

The Cruel Numbers of Love

Two to get in
And one
To get out:

Only one
To end
The entire rout.

So We'll Go No More

.

So it's fare thee well, my own true love:
I'm leaving you behind. And not
For the early, for the young reasons, but

For these late, last, ill reasons. I'm almost
Kaput! Yea, you'll get no more of me. . . .
Cancer, heart attack, bypass—all

In the same year? My chances
Are 20%! And I'm fucking well
Ready, ready to go. To go!—how often

I've operated that way. That way
Almost the entire caper, *the way*
For people, places, things:

Abandon, abandon, yea abandon before
Being abandoned . . . But we've, we've
Stayed . . . You the third wife for me, I

The second such boy for you, and I love
Looking directly into you, as we turn
Directly into this last get-go. We all

.

· *99* ·

Have the talent for leaving, like it
Or no. And oh, how rich it is, how fine
To finally *inherit*!: the final thing

I was looking for, as it turns *out*,
The great power of leaving
All the breathtakingly brief all along.

Cold and Soon

Cold and it is soon,
No matter what we think
(Or if we think at all).

Cold and soon now
We're headed off
To the warmer clime where

The food can be found.
Climb
This one last piece

Of mountain, over
Water, over plains
And desert where

We remember
The viscera of
Our climbing

Last season,
Flying this way
(For all we know)

One last time now.

Always

She liked to get high and go away.
She liked to get very high and go
Very far away. She would say

She was going to meet us
But then she wouldn't show up:
She'd gone very far away.

She knew it probably wasn't
The best thing to live this way but
She said she felt so much better

Whenever she stationed herself somewhere
Very far away, indeed as far away
As she could get from the bitter.

We begged her to stay, to stay and to stay
And to stay, and she took to mumbling
Something by Beckett, "Better abort

Than be barren," and then she'd go
Even farther away. She said she'd
Finally reached the point, after

Her husband died early and their daughter
Lost her mind, she'd finally reached the point
Where she'd just as soon

Go really far away. This was the point
Where we were getting intolerably tired
Of her turmoil (it was beginning

To involve money) and we threatened,
Ourselves, to go away.
Then she said she could easily see how

We'd reached this point, why we were
Beginning to feel that way, and she
Leaned into us to say she'd learned

Somewhere along the way
That abandonment, one way
Or the other, that abandonment

Was in the very mathematic of matter,
That abandonment, like it
Or not, really was the only way.

She said NO ONE GETS TO STAY.
And then she started rehearsing the story,
The story about being born,

Coming to fruition, and then having
To go away, and she said we'd really
Have to come to terms with this, that this

Was the way things went always, and as we
Started putting our coats on to leave she said
She wanted to thank us, that she'd been

Surprised and delighted, really surprised
And delighted, by just how long we had
Managed to stay. And when the call came

We decided the only way to put it,
The only way really to respond
To the "Why?" of it, was to say

She'd been walking along a precipice
For a very long time
And that she had slipped and managed

To go on over, and that was all,
About her going, that any of us
Could ever really say.

Soon the City

Soon the summer
Now the pleasant purgatory
Of spring is over,

Soon the choking
Humidity
In the city

On the fire escapes
In a sleeveless T-shirt
Smoking a cigar

In tune with the tremor
Of the mindless yellow
Commercial traffic

Moving in the city,
Where no one really
Buys a car,

American
Or otherwise,
Where we will,

·

As Rilke said we would,
Where we will
Wake, read, write

Long letters
And in the avenues
Wander restlessly

To and fro
On foot in
The humidity,

Where soon I'll shower, dress,
Take the dog out for a piss,
And mail this.